George Washington Carver

Other titles in the Inventors and Creators series include:

Inventors and Creators

George
Washington
Carver

Raymond H. Miller

KIDHAVEN PRESS

An imprint of Thomson Gale, a part of The Thomson Corporation

THOMSON
GALE

Detroit • New York • San Francisco • San Diego • New Haven, Conn. • Waterville, Maine • London • Munich

For more information, contact
KidHaven Press
27500 Drake Rd.
Farmington Hills, MI 48331-3535
Or you can visit our Internet site at http://www.gale.com

LIBRARY OF CONGRESS CATALOGING-IN-PUBLICATION DATA

Miller, Raymond H., 1967-
  George Washington Carver / by Raymond H. Miller.
    p. cm. — (Inventors and creators)
  Includes bibliographical references and index.
  ISBN 0-7377-3160-5 (hard cover : alk. paper)
  1. Carver, George Washington, 1864?-1943—Juvenile literature. 2. African American agriculturists—Biography—Juvenile literature. 3. Agriculturists—United States—Biography—Juvenile literature. I. Title. II. Series.
  S417.C3M536 2005
  630'.92—dc22
                                                     2004025832

Contents

Chapter One

Born into Slavery

George Washington Carver possessed one of the greatest scientific minds of his generation. His research at the Tuskegee Institute in Alabama in the late 19th century and the early 20th century led to breakthroughs that forever changed the farming industry in the South. Carver's achievements are all the more impressive because he faced **discrimination** most of his life simply because he was an African American. Despite this, he never gave up. He was determined to improve not only his own life, but also the lives of others in the African American community who shared his uphill battle to succeed in society.

Despite Carver's important achievements as an adult, his life began under humble and sometimes humiliating conditions. He was born a slave near Diamond Grove, Missouri, in either 1864 or 1865—no one knows for sure. The Civil War between the northern states, called the Union, and the southern states, called the Confederacy, was winding down, and slavery was nearing an end. George lived with his mother, Mary, and his older brother, James, on a farm owned by Moses Carver.

Moses and his wife, Susan, who were white, disagreed with the practice of slavery. However, they had purchased Mary from a neighbor because they needed help on their farm. The Carvers treated Mary and her two sons like family. They even gave Mary and her sons their last name. George never knew his father. It

As a young boy, George Washington Carver worked as a slave for a kindly master named Moses Carver.

is believed he was a slave on a neighbor's farm and was killed in an accident around the time of George's birth.

When George was very young, masked **raiders** kidnapped him and his mother and took them to Arkansas, where they planned to sell them to slave owners. Moses sent his neighbor to search for them and offered a racehorse as ransom. The neighbor found George and brought him home but could not locate Mary. Sadly, George and James never saw their mother again.

The Plant Doctor

George was nearly dead when the neighbor returned him to the Carvers. He was suffering from a severe fever and had the whooping cough, but the Carvers

George and his older brother, James, play marbles on the Carver homestead. The Carvers raised the boys as their own.

nursed him back to health. They took George and his brother into their home and raised them as their own. Although George recovered, his body remained weak for much of his childhood. He suffered from respiratory problems, which prevented him from doing hard work around the farm. He mainly helped Susan around the house. Some of his duties included mending clothes, cooking, and doing laundry. When he was healthy, he tended to the animals.

George loved being outdoors. He developed a strong interest in nature and spent much of his time exploring the woods close to the Carvers' house. He came to view the many elements of nature—rocks, trees, and animals—as evidence that God was everywhere. His faith in God remained strong all of his life. The Carvers encouraged his interest in nature by letting him plant a small garden.

George found fascinating the conditions under which the plants grew best. If a plant did not grow well, he tried giving it more water or moving it into the sunlight. He became such an expert gardener that residents of Diamond Grove called him the "plant doctor."

A Desire to Learn

George demonstrated a strong desire to learn by spending hours each day studying his plants. He wanted to go to the school near the Carvers' home so he could learn how to read and write, but only white children were allowed to attend the school. This was one of George's earliest memories of **racism**. Even though George believed this was unfair, he did his best not to complain.

This creek running through the Carver homestead was one of the many outdoor places young George liked to explore.

Sensing George's frustration, Susan found an old *Webster's Elementary Spelling Book* in the attic and gave it to George. She taught him the letters of the alphabet, and he soon learned how to read. He read the spelling book from cover to cover, yet it could not provide the answers to his questions. "I wanted to know the name of every stone and flower and insect and bird and beast," he later said. "I wanted to know where it got its color, where it got its life—but there was no one to tell me." [1]

George wanted to learn from a teacher in a real classroom, not from an old spelling book. He decided that if he was not allowed to join the students attending class at the school in Diamond Grove, he would do the next best thing. Each morning he walked to the school and sat on the front steps, from where he could hear the lesson through an open window. When George was ten years old, he learned the town of Neosho, which was 8 miles (12.9km) away, had a school just for black children. He pleaded with the Carvers to let him attend the school, but Neosho was too far away for George to walk every day. George would have to wait a few more years until he was old enough to set out on his own.

The next year, the Carvers paid a private tutor named Steven Slane to teach George, but before long, George was asking questions even Slane could not answer. When George was twelve, Moses and Susan finally decided it was time to let him go to Neosho. George could barely contain his excitement knowing he was going to receive an education at a real school.

The Lincoln School

The first person he met in Neosho was an African American woman named Mariah Watkins. She and her husband, Andrew, did not have children of their own and were happy to let George stay with them. Mariah had him help her with household chores, such as sewing and doing laundry. He also spent much of his time reading from a *Bible* that Mariah had given him for Christmas.

The school in Neosho that George attended was called the Lincoln School. Class was held in an old shack crowded with more than 70 students. George did not mind the difficult conditions as long as he

George spent much of his time reading from this *Bible* that Mariah Watkins gave him one Christmas.

could learn more about his favorite topic, plants. However, George's teacher had a limited education and, like George's former tutor, did not have all the answers to his questions.

George was just thirteen years old when he realized it was time to move on. He told Mariah that he was going to search for a school that could teach him the things he wanted to know. Before he left, however, she made him promise that he would one day teach other African American children who were also eager to learn.

Chapter Two

Wandering Ways

E ven though the Civil War brought an end to slavery, many former slaves could not find jobs or go to school in the South. A large number of them began moving to areas where more opportunities existed. George believed the state of Kansas offered a better chance for him to further his education. In 1878, he moved to Fort Scott, Kansas, and lived with the family of Felix Payne, a blacksmith.

George cooked and cleaned for the Paynes in exchange for room and board. To earn money, he worked across the street at a grocery store and took in laundry from guests at a local hotel. He used some of the money to purchase books so he could attend school.

While in Fort Scott, George witnessed an act of racism that affected him the rest of his life. One day in the spring of 1879, an African American man was accused of attacking a white girl. After sundown, a group of white men removed the man from prison. George witnessed the mob tie a rope around the accused man, drag him by the neck, and hang him from

Lucy Seymour and her husband Ben welcomed George into their home while he worked odd jobs in Olathe, Kansas.

a lamppost. The hanging so terrified George that he left Fort Scott immediately. "As young as I was," Carver recalled more than 60 years later, "the horror haunted me and does even now." [2]

After leaving Fort Scott, George settled in Olathe, Kansas, where he lived with another African American couple named Ben and Lucy Seymour. He did odd jobs, such as shining shoes, and also cooked and cleaned for the local barber's family. On Sundays, he taught a class at the Methodist church in Olathe. Soon, however, George was on the move again. When the Seymours moved to Minneapolis, Kansas, he traveled with them.

Chasing a Dream

Once in Minneapolis, George turned his household skills into a business opportunity. He borrowed $156.45 from a bank and opened a laundry service in a small shack in a poor part of Minneapolis known as "Poverty Gulch." George invited friends to the shack and entertained them with stories.

One of George's favorite stories was how he got his middle name. He informed friends that while living in Minneapolis he began receiving the mail of a man also named George Carver. So that others could tell the two men apart, George decided to add a *W* to his name. He told his friends the *W* stood for Washington. From that moment on, he was known as George Washington Carver.

As always, George also found plenty of time to devote to his education. He attended high school in a four-room, two-story schoolhouse in Minneapolis, but this time, he was allowed to attend with white students. He impressed his classmates with his strong knowledge of science, history, and other subjects, including art and music. He learned how to paint beautiful flowers and became an accomplished harmonica and accordion player.

By 1884, George was out of school and setting his sights on college. He quickly learned how unlikely a dream this was when he applied by mail to Highland College in Highland, Kansas. The college accepted him, but when he arrived for registration, he was turned away because he was African American. George was disappointed and decided to put off going to college.

In 1886, George moved to Beeler, Kansas, and bought a large but inexpensive piece of land from the government. He built a **sod house** out of chunks of soil and grass, grew his own vegetables, and kept hens. Even though most of the people in Beeler were white, George was welcomed into the community. However, he was not satisfied in Beeler. The cold Kansas winters made farming difficult, and he was also eager to resume his search for a college that would accept him. Sometime in the late 1880s, he moved to Winterset, Iowa.

College Finally

In Winterset, Carver worked at the St. Nicholas Hotel and opened another laundry service. He also attended church in town, where he met a wealthy couple, the Millhollands, who would change his life. They were impressed with Carver's intelligence and artistic ability and urged him to enter Simpson College, a small Methodist school in nearby Indianola, Iowa. Carver was happy to learn Simpson College admitted students of every race. He applied to the school and was accepted. Carver was thrilled to finally be going to college.

Though Carver was the only black student enrolled at Simpson College, the other students warmly accepted him and even bought a table, chairs, and a bed for his

George created this detailed oil painting of white lilies while he was still in high school.

room. They also slipped money under his door when he needed it. "They made me believe I was a real human being,"[3] he recalled.

Carver's studies included arithmetic, essay writing, grammar, piano, and voice lessons, but where he truly excelled was in an art class taught by a young woman named Etta Budd. Carver and Budd developed a close friendship. Under her guidance, he became an accomplished painter. He loved to paint scenes from nature, particularly flowers. His paintings were so good that he entered some of them in Chicago's 1893 World's Fair and won honorable mention.

In talking to Carver and studying the detail of his paintings, Budd soon realized Carver had a brilliant mind for **horticulture**, the art and science of growing fruits, vegetables, and other plants. She suggested he transfer to Iowa State College of Agriculture and Mechanic Arts (now Iowa State University), where her father was a professor of horticulture. Convinced that God had great work for him to do in agriculture, he took her advice and applied to the college. Again, he was accepted.

An Energetic Student

Carver was eager to begin his studies at Iowa State, though as the only African American on campus, he endured ridicule from some of the students early on. Carver won over disapproving students with his likable personality and became an accepted part of the student body. He actively participated in many campus activities by joining the Welsh Eclectic Society (a debating club), the German Club, and the Art Club.

He organized the Agricultural Society, arranged prayer meetings, and was the trainer for the college's football team. Carver also served in the campus military regiment and became a captain, the highest rank.

Iowa State provided an excellent opportunity for Carver to hone his skills as a horticulturalist. The school, a leader in agricultural research, employed some of the best professors in the field. In the classroom, Carver was highly regarded by his professors for his knowledge of plant **grafting** and **cross-fertilization**, techniques that involved using two plants to grow a

Carver's Iowa State College creamery operators class poses for a portrait. Carver (back row, second from right) studied horticulture at the all-white college.

single, but improved, plant. In his favorite subjects, he earned between a 3.9 and a perfect 4.0 grade point average. Carver received his college degree in 1894. He then began working toward his Master of Agriculture degree. While taking the advanced courses, he joined the Iowa State faculty as a biology assistant. This allowed him to teach freshman courses. Carver thrived in his new role as teacher.

Then in March 1896, Carver received a letter from a nationally known African American leader named Booker T. Washington. Washington was the principal of the Tuskegee Institute, a school in Alabama that emphasized vocational training for African American students. Washington wanted Carver to come to Tuskegee as the head of the new Department of Agriculture. Carver was very happy at Iowa State, but after much persuasion from Washington, he finally accepted the offer. Carver was excited at the opportunity to move to the South and share his knowledge with his fellow African Americans, just as Mariah Watkins had hoped many years earlier.

Chapter Three

The Wizard of Tuskegee

Carver stayed at Iowa State long enough to finish his studies. After receiving his master's degree, he left Iowa and arrived in Tuskegee in the fall of 1896. He believed God had a divine purpose for his life, and he viewed his move to Alabama as a kind of mission to help the African Americans living there.

Despite his excitement, Carver had never lived in the Deep South, and he was unprepared for what he faced when he arrived there. Even though slavery had ended decades earlier, African Americans were still thought of in the South as secondary citizens. They had few social or political rights, and many were sickly because they did not eat or have access to healthy foods. Carver knew he had to help them.

Carver and Booker T. Washington believed African Americans would become an accepted part of society only if they could prove their usefulness to the southern economy. The two men saw the Tuskegee

In 1896 Booker T. Washington (pictured) invited Carver to run the Department of Agriculture at the Tuskegee Institute in Alabama.

Institute as a perfect way for African Americans to receive an education and begin contributing to society, but the task of turning an uneducated group of people into productive workers would be difficult for Carver.

Unlike Iowa State, the Tuskegee Institute was not a modern academic center. It combined the functions of an elementary school, a high school, and a vocational school. The Department of Agriculture received just $1,500 a year in educational funds from the state of Alabama. Carver's first classroom was an old blacksmith's shop.

Despite the school's lack of facilities and supplies, Carver was committed to helping his students receive the best education he and the school could offer. He formed strong bonds with his students and affectionately called them "my children." They in turn called him "prof." He also showed his love and concern for them by occasionally lending money to the poorest ones when they needed it.

Another way Carver hoped to see students succeed was to make education a creative, hands-on experience. Sometimes this was necessary because of the school's lack of modern equipment. Once, he and his students constructed a science laboratory almost exclusively from various items they collected from garbage cans and junkyards around the neighborhood.

Saving Cotton

Carver's responsibilities went far beyond just teaching. As head of the school's Department of Agriculture, he was also responsible for the two school farms. These included the barns and animals, the dairy, a poultry yard, and of course the many fields in which he grew and tested fruit and vegetable **crops**. He used the homemade science lab to analyze soil samples around Tuskegee.

Carver quickly learned that by planting cotton year after year in the same fields, the farmers had depleted important nutrients and elements, including nitrogen, from the soil. The sickly cotton plants proved this. He knew that a change was needed or the cotton industry was likely to fail, which would further damage the struggling southern economy. First he had his students plow the cotton plants under the soil. He then had them grow sweet potatoes, which also improved soil conditions by putting nitrogen back into the earth. The next year they grew cowpeas, which grew in abundance. Carver could see his experiment was working.

In the third year, the students went back to planting cotton. They were thrilled when their plants grew amazingly well. Carver had discovered that **crop rotation**, or growing different crops in the field each year, replenished the soil with the missing components. This resulted in healthier plants.

Carver also grew a gigantic pumpkin vine using soil from a **compost** pile he had developed from food scraps. This dramatic effect demonstrated how poor African American farmers could make their own organic fertilizer for free. People started calling Carver the "Wizard of Tuskegee."

Early in his research, Carver discovered the soil conditions necessary for growing healthy plants like this cotton.

Carver showed poor African American farmers how to use their compost as fertilizer.

A Farmer's Best Friend

Carver immediately put his experiments into practice by sharing them with African American farmers around Tuskegee. He set up monthly meetings and called them the Farmer's Institute. By the early 1900s, Carver was receiving wide acclaim for his work.

Soon African American farmers came to Tuskegee from all over the South to hear Carver's revolutionary ideas. They listened to Carver give lectures about the science of farming, including crop rotation and organic fertilizers, as well as **hybridization** techniques he had developed. This complex process involved crossing two different plants to enhance the best qualities of each one. Plant hybrids were resistant to disease and drought and produced a large crop.

Carver also used the meetings to help people save money and to address the problem of malnutrition. He showed the farmers how to turn cowpeas into variations of cornbread, meatloaf, and pancakes. He demonstrated how, instead of having to buy laundry starch, flour, and syrup, they could make these things from sweet potatoes.

In 1906, Carver took his ideas on the road after receiving materials for a mobile laboratory station from

Touring the South in his mechanized version of the Jesup Agricultural Wagon, a kind of mobile laboratory, Carver shared his ideas with local farmers.

a wealthy New York banker named Morris K. Jesup. Carver named the school's laboratory-on-wheels the Jesup Agricultural Wagon. The wagon displayed different types of dairy equipment and included charts on how to develop fertile soil, raise healthy livestock, and more. Carver hauled the wagon to cotton patches, cornfields, and country stores throughout the South. Word of the Jesup Wagon's success reached Washington, D.C.

The U.S. Department of Agriculture began funding the program and Carver became the first African American to be named a government demonstration agent. Carver was pleased to be funded by the U.S. government to travel the countryside and share his equipment and expertise with farmers.

After Carver had spent nearly ten years at the Tuskegee Institute, people all over the nation had come to respect and admire him. His work had done much to solve many of the problems that for years had been plaguing the southern farming industry and African Americans in general. The agricultural programs he helped establish at the school became the envy of every college attended primarily by African Americans in the South.

Trouble at Tuskegee

Despite Carver's celebrity, he experienced his share of disappointments and setbacks. His relationship with Booker T. Washington, for example, was less than perfect. Both men had strong personalities, and each had his own opinion on how Carver could best help African Americans.

Pictured is the laboratory equipment Carver used to perform his invaluable experiments.

Carver wanted to spend most of his time out on the road, as he had been doing with the Jesup Wagon. But Washington wanted his young teacher back at Tuskegee full-time, where he could focus on teaching and tending to his administrative duties. Carver enjoyed teaching, but he favored research over the many responsibilities that came with being head of the department. As principal, Washington increased Carver's workload and demanded that the Department of Agriculture be run more efficiently.

More problems began to mount when Washington hired a young teacher named George R. Bridgeforth to assist Carver with his duties. The two men quarreled almost constantly, increasing Carver's unhappiness at Tuskegee. Carver frequently complained to Washington about Bridgeforth, but time and time again, Washington sided with Bridgeforth. After being laid off for an entire month during the summer of 1914, Carver no longer felt appreciated at the school. He threatened to resign, yet he could not bring himself to leave. He believed he still had important work to do.

Chapter Four

Growing Goobers

A s Carver's ongoing feud with Bridgeforth contin-ued to put a strain on his relationship with Wash-ington, he gradually retreated from his responsibilities at Tuskegee. Though he maintained a presence at the school, he began to focus on his research off campus. He built another mobile laboratory with whatever parts he could scavenge and called it "God's little workshop."

Several years later, Carver became friends with the famous automobile maker, Henry Ford, who gave Carver the funding to build a new laboratory. Carver was able to use the modern equipment to perfect the process of removing rubber from the milk of the gold-enrod plant, which Ford hoped to use in automobile tires. As always, however, Carver had a strong desire to help African Americans in the South, and he used the laboratory to continue his work in improving crops.

In November 1915, Washington died unexpect-edly. Though Carver and Washington often disagreed, Carver deeply respected the principal. In the months following Washington's death, Carver was filled with

In the early 1900s, Carver became friends with automobile maker Henry Ford (right).

sadness. His thoughts were focused mainly on the arguments between the two men, forgetting many of the good times they had shared. "I am sure Mr. Washington never knew how much I loved him," he wrote later, "and the cause [of helping African Americans] for which he gave his life." [4]

Plant Peanuts

After Washington's death, Carver seemed to step out of the great African American leader's shadow. He began to receive more appreciation for his contributions to the agriculture industry than ever before. In 1916, he was invited to join the advisory board of the National Agricultural Society. That same year he became the only African American member of Great Britain's Royal Society for the Encouragement of the Arts, one of the country's most prestigious scientific societies. Two years later, he was appointed as a consultant to the U.S. Department of Agriculture. He later received the Springarn Medal for Distinguished Service to science and the Theodore Roosevelt Medal for his contributions to agriculture.

A few years before his death, Carver donated his life savings to Tuskegee to help others continue his important research.

In the course of his research, Carver devised more than 300 uses for the peanut plant (pictured).

Much of Carver's fame had come from his research on peanut plants earlier in his career at the Tuskegee Institute. African slaves had brought the peanut plant to the United States in the 18th and 19th centuries. They called peanuts "goobers," a term derived from the African word for peanut, *nguba*. However, goobers were not very popular in the early 1900s. People called them "monkey food" because they were often fed to animals. Carver changed all that when he was out in a field examining sickly cotton plants and noticed healthy peanut plants growing beside them. Carver told farmers to plow the cotton plants into the soil and plant peanuts instead. The farmers were hesitant, but they eventually did when he explained to them his theory on crop rotation.

Addressing Congress

The peanut plants grew so well that soon the farmers came to Carver with another problem. There were too many peanuts. Carver had no answers for them at the time, so he went to work in his laboratory. Some time later, Carver invited several businessmen to have dinner with them. He served them bread, soup, meat, cookies, and ice cream. He received many compliments. The guests were shocked when Carver told them he had made everything from peanuts. He later discovered that peanuts could be turned into margarine, cooking oil, rubbing oil, and cosmetics. In all, Carver came up with more than 300 uses for peanuts.

The peanut industry incorporated Carver's research, and goober success swept the nation. By 1920, growers in the South formed the United Peanut Association of America. Carver gave a speech at their first annual convention. But then trouble began. Peanuts being shipped to the United States were threatening the nation's peanut industry because they were so inexpensive. Peanut growers in the South were having a hard time competing with the low prices of their foreign competitors.

Carver convinced farmers to practice crop rotation by plowing their cotton plants into the soil and grow peanuts instead.

To help the farmers, Carver spoke before the U.S. Congress. He hoped to convince Congress to increase the price of peanuts being imported into the United States from other countries. Carver thought most of the nation's peanuts should come from peanut growers at home, which would benefit the South. He was given just ten minutes to talk, but that turned into an hour when the congressmen continued to sit spellbound listening to the soft-spoken man. In the end, Congress voted to increase the price of peanuts from other countries, saving the U.S. peanut industry.

Miracle Oil

By the late 1920s, Carver had scaled back many of his administrative duties at Tuskegee. He taught only summer courses and held Sunday night *Bible* classes. He devoted the rest of his time to fulfilling his dream of helping others.

One of the ways Carver sought to make people's lives better was by developing a special massage oil using peanut oil. He believed that just as cowpeas and sweet potatoes improved soil conditions by restoring missing elements, peanut oil could replenish the body with minerals it was lacking. When a frail and severely underweight boy gained 31 pounds (14.06kg) in one month, Carver believed he had found proof that peanuts could heal people.

Carver traveled around Alabama giving speeches that hinted at a possibility for other cures. Two polio patients he treated with the peanut oil massages also responded well. Soon Carver's "miracle oil" was featured on the front page of many newspapers. Hundreds of people suffering from various diseases and ailments began writing to Carver asking for help.

In 1939, Carver's own health began to deteriorate. He was unable to start any new research or set out on many lecturing trips. Instead, he donated his life savings, $33,000, to establish the George Washington Carver Foundation at Tuskegee so others could con-

Shown here at work in his Tuskegee lab, Carver is today
known as one of the foremost agricultural chemists in history.

tinue his important research. This was an action that supported his personal goals: "I am not a finisher. I am a blazer of trails. . . . Others must take up the various trails of truth, and carry them on." [5] The facility opened in 1941, completing his last and perhaps most rewarding work in the field of agriculture.

Carver fell ill in late 1942 and died on January 5, 1943. The Tuskegee Institute was flooded with cards, telegrams, and letters from celebrities, schoolchildren, scientists, and especially farmers. Funeral services held at the Tuskegee chapel overflowed with people of every race and many different walks of life. The outpouring of affection and admiration was evidence that Carver had become a legend and folk hero not only to African American southerners, but to people everywhere.

Notes

Chapter 1: Born into Slavery
1. Quoted in Edwin E. Sparks, "The Wizard of the Goober and the Yam," *American Life*, November 1923, p. 14.

Chapter 2: Wandering Ways
2. Quoted in Robert P. Fuller and Merrill J. Mattes, "The Early Life of George Washington Carver," *GWC Papers* at Tuskegee Institute Archives, 1957, p. 29.

3. Quoted in Linda O. McMurry, *George Washington Carver: Scientist & Symbol.* New York: Oxford, 1981, p. 28.

Chapter 4: Growing Goobers
4. Quoted in McMurry, *George Washington Carver*, p. 159.

5. Quoted in Leavell, "The Boy Who Was Traded for a Horse," *Baptist Student*, November 1938, p. 6.

Glossary

compost: A mixture of decayed organic matter used for fertilizing plants.

crop rotation: Growing different plants in a field each year to replenish the soil.

crops: The plants a farmer grows in a single season.

cross-fertilization: The crossing of two different plants to create a new one.

discrimination: The unfair treatment of a person because of his or her race.

grafting: The joining of two plants together so they grow as one.

horticulture: The science and art of growing plants.

hybridization: The act of producing a plant by breeding two different varieties of the plant.

racism: The act of discriminating against someone based solely on the person's race.

raiders: A group of violent robbers.

sod house: A house popular during the pioneer days that was made of chunks of soil and grass.

For Further Exploration

Books

David A. Adler and Dan Brown, *A Picture Book of George Washington Carver*. New York: Holiday House, 2000. Documents Carver's life in pictures and examines many of his important contributions to science.

Margo McLoone, *George Washington Carver*. Mankato, MN: Bridgestone, 1997. A photo-illustrated biography of Carver, complete with a chronological listing of his important achievements.

Eva Moore, *The Story of George Washington Carver*. New York: Scholastic, 1995. Explores the key events that shaped Carver's life in an easy-to-read style.

Web Sites

George Washington Carver National Monument (www.nps.gov/gwca). The official Web site of the Carver National Monument, which includes the boyhood home of George Washington Carver.

The Legacy of George Washington Carver (www.lib.iastate.edu/spcl/gwc/home.html). A Web site maintained by Iowa State University, Carver's alma mater. Includes a biography as well as excellent resources, such as a painting, a poem, and his famous 1925 bulletin about growing peanuts.

Index

Picture Credits

About the Author

Raymond H. Miller is the author of more than 50 nonfiction books for children. He has written on a range of topics from poisonous animals to presidential trivia. He enjoys playing sports and spending time outdoors with his wife and two daughters.